Beyond the Veil:

A Journey Through Near Death Experiences

John Martin Dewane

Studio of Books LLC
5900 Balcones Drive Suite 100
Austin, Texas 78731
www.studioofbooks.org
Hotline: (254) 800-1183

Ordering Information:
Special discounts are available on quantity purchases by corporations, associations, and others. For details, contact the publisher at the address above.

Printed in the United States of America.

ISBN-13:   Softcover   978-1-964864-79-2
                eBook   978-1-964864-80-8

Library of Congress Control Number: 2024923991

Dedication

In loving memory of my late Uncle Jorge Dewane, whose unwavering support, boundless curiosity, and profound wisdom inspired me to write "Beyond the Veil." Your memory remains a source of strength and your belief in me continues to guide my journey.

Acknowledgment

I would like to express my deepest gratitude to the individuals who stood by my side during my challenging journey while writing "Beyond the Veil." Their unwavering support and love have been instrumental in bringing this book to fruition.

First and foremost, I want to thank my partner, Walter Blasberg, for his unwavering presence and encouragement throughout my stay in the hospital. Your love and strength gave me the determination to keep pushing forward, even during the toughest times.

I am eternally grateful to my mother, Aida Dewane, whose constant presence and care brought me immense comfort during my hospitalization. Your unwavering love and sacrifices are beyond measure, and I am truly blessed to have you as my mother.

A heartfelt appreciation goes to my nephew, Sergio Junior, who traveled all the way to Vermont to drive my mother and support her while I was unable to. Your selflessness and willingness to lend a helping hand touched my heart deeply.

I would also like to extend my thanks to all my siblings, friends, and family who kept me in their prayers, both in the United States and in Mexico and Honduras. Your thoughts and well-wishes gave me strength and hope during the most challenging moments of my journey.

A special mention goes to my cousins, Juan Carlos and Roberto Jose, whose emotional response upon learning of my illness reminded me of the importance of love and connection. Your tears and concern touched my soul, and I am grateful for your support.

To my grandnephew, Isiah Gomez, whose innocent plea for me not to leave this world was a powerful reminder of the impact we can have on each other's lives, thank you. Your words of hope and your promise to be there for me pushed me to fight harder.

I would also like to acknowledge the University of Vermont Medical Center priest who provided me with spiritual guidance and administered the last rites. Your presence brought me solace and peace during a challenging time.

A special thank you goes to Gary Rudin, whose visits and guitar playing brought joy and light into my hospital room. Your talent and thoughtfulness lifted my spirits, and I will always cherish those moments.

Furthermore, I would like to extend my gratitude to all those who visited me in the hospital, even though I was unable to consciously be there to see them or engage in conversation. Your presence brought comfort to my loved ones, and the knowledge that you took the time to visit meant the world to me. Your support and well-wishes uplifted my spirits and contributed to my healing process.

A special mention goes to my dear friend, Nancy Blasberg. Your willingness to read my work and provide insightful feedback was a tremendous gift. Your suggestions and guidance helped me enhance the depth and clarity of my writing. I am grateful for your friendship and unwavering support throughout this creative journey.

Last but not least, I want to express my profound appreciation to Dr. Elizabeth Blasberg. Your dedication and support, even during your precious time off from your studies, touched me deeply. Your expertise and care were invaluable in my recovery, and I am forever grateful.

Beyond the Veil:

A Journey Through Near Death Experiences

To all the individuals who played a part, whether big or small, in the creation and completion of "Beyond the Veil," please accept my heartfelt thanks. Your contributions, whether through personal support, professional expertise, or critical feedback, have made this book a reality. I am forever grateful for your presence in my life.

With sincere appreciation,

John Martin Dewane

Table of Contents

About the Author

John Martin Dewane's story begins on April 3, 1969, in San Pedro Sula, Honduras, born to Aida Dewane and Oscar Vidal Martinez. Growing up in Honduras, John completed his primary education, concluding his sixth-grade studies in November 1981. Shortly thereafter, his parents made the pivotal decision to relocate the family to the United States in pursuit of greater educational and professional opportunities.

Adapting to a new environment posed numerous challenges for John upon his arrival in the United States. Despite the tumultuous nature of his upbringing, he exhibited unwavering resilience and determination in forging a successful path forward. At the age of 18, John ventured out, relocating to Chicago, where he dedicated himself to establishing a career within the financial sector.

Commencing his professional journey as a customer service representative at an international bank, John's diligence and dedication propelled him swiftly through the ranks. His natural leadership and business acumen saw him rise to the role of operations supervisor, marking the onset of a remarkable career trajectory.

Understanding the significance of education in achieving his long-term aspirations, John embarked on a path of higher learning while balancing the demands of his burgeoning career. Evenings were dedicated to pursuing studies at DePaul University, with a pivotal decision to relocate to New York City with just one semester remaining in his educational pursuits.

It was in the bustling backdrop of New York City that John successfully completed his studies at Fordham University, earning a degree in Economics. This achievement stood as a testament to his expertise in the field, positioning him for continued success within the financial industry.

Armed with his academic accomplishments and a solid financial background, John secured a position with Citicorp, a renowned financial institution. This role granted him extensive travel opportunities across the United States and later expanded to encompass journeys throughout South America, broadening his global perspective and enriching his professional tenure.

In 1999, John took a momentous career shift, transitioning out of the financial realm to join forces with his partner at The North Hero House Inn and Restaurant. Embracing the role of an innkeeper, John infused innovative ideas and business acumen, propelling the establishment, alongside his partner, into a thriving enterprise.

His personal journey reached a significant milestone in 2005 when John Martin Dawani became a naturalized citizen of the United States, solidifying his commitment to his adopted homeland and embracing his identity as an American citizen.

The transformative turning point in John's life came on May 15th, 2010, when he made the life-altering decision to take his last alcoholic beverage, signaling the commencement of his journey towards sobriety. The following day, he voluntarily admitted himself to the Brattleboro Retreat for detoxification, displaying immense courage and determination to lead an alcohol-free life.

In 2012, John faced a medical crisis during a routine gall bladder surgery at the University of Vermont Medical Center. Unexpected complications left him in critical condition, eventually facing hospice paperwork. It was amidst this tumultuous period that John underwent a near-death experience (NDE), a profound encounter that would fundamentally alter his perspective on life and spirituality.

Surviving the challenges posed by the gall bladder surgery, John emerged imbued with a renewed sense of purpose and an unwavering determination to effect positive change. In May 2017, he embarked on a new chapter, founding the Angels for Honduras foundation (http://www.aph1.org), dedicated to empowering underprivileged children and orphans in

Honduras by providing access to education, catalyzing transformative change in their lives and futures.

Through this foundation, John directed his steadfast commitment to philanthropy and his belief in the transformative power of education. The mission to offer educational opportunities to disadvantaged children aligns with his enduring dedication to create a brighter, more equitable future for the youth of Honduras.

In his personal life, John Martin Dewane finds solace amidst the natural beauty of North Hero, Vermont, during the summer months, while winters are spent in West Palm Beach, Florida, alongside his partner, Walter, and his mother, Aida, fostering a nurturing environment. The household is further enriched by the presence of cherished pets, adding joy and companionship to their lives.

John's multifaceted journey, characterized by resilience, reinvention, and an unwavering dedication to philanthropy, stands as a testament to the transformative nature of personal growth and the pursuit of a purpose-driven life. His initiatives through the Angels for Honduras foundation exemplify his commitment to effecting positive change and uplifting the lives of others, embodying values of compassion, empathy, and empowerment.

Introduction

"Beyond the Veil" is an exhilarating journey into the unknown territories of near-death experiences (NDEs), crafted by the insightful John Martin Dewane. Through a captivating blend of personal narratives and meticulous research, Dewane beckons readers to venture into a realm where life and what lies beyond intertwine, revealing the secrets of our existence.

In this odyssey, readers are invited to explore the depths of consciousness and spirituality, where Dewane skillfully dissects recurring themes in NDEs. He compellingly argues for the existence of an afterlife and the timeless essence of the soul, guiding us through the stages of these extraordinary encounters—from departing the physical body to encountering departed loved ones and ethereal beings.

Dewane takes us on a multidimensional ride, examining NDEs through scientific, spiritual, and philosophical lenses. Infused with empathy, he shares how these experiences ignite personal growth and purpose. Inspired by his own NDE, Dewane founded the Angeles Para Honduras foundation, illuminating the transformative power of such profound moments.

Beyond the Veil:

A Journey Through Near Death Experiences

This book seamlessly melds personal anecdotes, scientific insights, and spiritual wisdom, painting a vivid picture of the enigmatic afterlife. From life reviews to encounters with higher powers, it plunges into the depths of human consciousness, igniting contemplation about the limitless potential beyond the ordinary.

"Beyond the Veil" isn't just an eye-opener—it's an invitation to challenge perceptions and ponder life's true essence. It stands as a guiding beacon for those seeking enlightenment about the afterlife, offering hope, inspiration, and a profound understanding of the life-altering impact of near-death experiences.

Chapter 1: A Glimpse into the Unknown

Introduction to near-death experiences (NDEs) and their significance:

Near-death experiences (NDEs) stand as enigmatic gateways, opening a window to a realm that remains beyond the grasp of our understanding. These moments, occurring on the precipice of life and death, carry individuals through a profound odyssey that defies the limitations of our physical world.

Imagine drifting beyond the confines of your body, suspended in an ethereal realm, gazing upon the scene of your own medical emergency. Witnesses to these experiences often recount the surreal sensation of watching doctors and nurses toil fervently, attempting to reclaim their slipping hold on life.

But it's not just the sights; it's the sensations that paint the canvas of an NDE. There's a prevalent narrative of a serene, radiant light, an illumination that surpasses any earthly brilliance, suffusing the surroundings with an all-encompassing warmth and an overwhelming sense of love—an emotion beyond measure or comparison.

Yet, it doesn't end there. Departed loved ones often make an appearance, offering solace or guidance, blurring the lines between this world and the next. Some even speak of a life review, a cinematic reel where every moment, every choice, every emotion is relived, presenting a profound introspection that transcends the ordinary.

These encounters leave an indelible mark, transforming individuals in ways that language struggles to capture. Priorities shift, beliefs are reshaped, and perspectives undergo a seismic shift. It's this transformation, this metamorphosis of the soul, that underscores the profound significance of near-death experiences. They beckon us to contemplate the nature of existence, the enigma of life and death, and the possibility of an existence beyond what we perceive.

Personal background and the moment of receiving hospice papers:

June 8th, 2012. A date that stands as the genesis of a tumultuous journey, marked by unexpected twists that would redefine my existence. Little did I anticipate that a seemingly routine gall bladder surgery at the University of Vermont Medical Center would thrust me into an uncharted territory of despair and resilience.

As the operation commenced, unawareness shielded me from the unfolding catastrophe that awaited. The operating room bustled with activity while I lay there, oblivious to the impending storm. But fate had other plans—something went grievously wrong during the procedure, hurling me into the throes of critical care in the ICU.

In those initial moments, my partner remained blissfully unaware of the gravity of the situation. Assured by the doctors that all was well, he departed, unwitting of the battle I was waging for my very life. My world, cloaked in pain and fear, blurred amidst the constant cacophony of beeping monitors and the sterile surroundings of medical apparatus.

Days stretched into an eternity, my condition teetering on the edge of oblivion. The medical team waged a relentless war to stabilize me, to undo the havoc wreaked by the surgery gone awry. Each passing moment was an agonizing uncertainty, a test of endurance and hope.

Then came the moment etched in the contours of despair. Dr. Neil Hyman, his solemn countenance a harbinger of grim tidings, approached my partner. The weight of his words painted a dire picture—my liver, a vital sentinel, had turned traitor, unleashing havoc upon my body. Organs ravaged, I was ensnared in the clutches of sepsis, my existence hanging by a precarious thread.

Beyond the Veil:
A Journey Through Near Death Experiences

Weeks unfurled in a haze of excruciating pain and relentless procedures. Endoscopies sought to rectify the damage, tubes snaked within me, draining the vile bile that sought to devour my very being. It was a maddening race against time, a battle where agony was a constant companion, etching its presence into every fiber of my being.

But the struggle did not cease. Tubes invaded, medications numbed, and my body bore the scars of this relentless ordeal. The medical fraternity scoured for answers, each test, each consultation a desperate attempt to decode the enigma of my illness.

Returning home, the familiar surroundings belied the toll my body had endured. Gaunt and fragile, my reflection in the mirror was an unrecognizable echo of my former self. The battle scars of a prolonged hospital stay etched a narrative of anguish upon my physique.

Yet, just as hope dared to flicker, a fresh tribulation emerged. Eating, once an instinctual act, became a Herculean task. Every meal was a gamble, a perilous tightrope walk between sustenance and rejection. The weight plummeted, and with it, the spirit faltered.

Days blurred into a vortex of challenges, my body succumbing to a relentless decline. The inability to keep nourishment down became a looming specter, a relentless tormentor mocking the fragility of my existence.

In the midst of this turmoil, tragedy struck again. On July 11th, my faithful companion, Oscar, departed from this world, leaving behind an irreparable void. His loss compounded the emotional turmoil, his absence a dark cloud eclipsing an already arduous journey.

Yet, in the depths of grief, I saw a glimmer—a belief that Oscar's sacrifice shielded me from deeper despair. His spirit became a beacon, guiding me through the shadows, reminding me of the resilience I carried within.

The pain of loss lingered, but I refused to be consumed. With each passing day, I channeled grief into resilience, weaving Oscar's love into the fabric of my determination.

Amidst the relentless pain, my mind became a treacherous landscape. Hallucinations danced, reality and imagination merged, painting a disorienting canvas of surreal experiences. Yet, amidst the chaos, I clung to a flicker of sanity, a resolve to emerge from this labyrinth, unscathed.

In a morphine-induced haze, an ethereal encounter emerged—a vision of my departed uncle, Jorge. His presence,

Beyond the Veil:

A Journey Through Near Death Experiences

a testament to wisdom and reassurance, offered guidance in the midst of my delirium. His words, a soothing balm, reaffirmed my purpose, breathing new life into my embattled spirit.

As the hallucination dissolved, a renewed determination surged. I made a vow—no surrender to pain, addiction, or despair. My voice, a vessel of conviction, echoed defiance in the face of seemingly insurmountable odds.

However, the resolute spirit clashed with a body that continued to betray. Amidst the medications, a stark reminder emerged—the hospice papers, a stark verdict from a medical system seemingly resigned.

Yet, in the embrace of loved ones, hope persisted. Their unwavering belief, a lifeline amidst desolation, fueled a refusal to yield. Even as the medical verdict loomed, a spark of intuition stirred.

Research led to a potential solution—a barium enema. A hesitant attempt brought unexpected rumblings within. A glimmer of hope dawned, prompting a return to the hospital, a fragile anticipation of a breakthrough.

Days unfurled, hope warred with uncertainty, until a moment of revelation—a half sandwich and water stayed down. A tentative victory emerged, a fragile beacon amidst the encroaching darkness.

However, the journey took another unexpected turn—hospitalization, fever, and dwindling blood pressure. Diagnosis unveiled an infection, a consequence of earlier afflictions. A renewed battle ensued, met with a fortified spirit and unwavering support.

Treatment and resilience prevailed. Fever subsided, blood pressure stabilized—a testament to the resilience of the human spirit amidst adversity. Discharged from the hospital, I returned home, a convergence of relief, gratitude, and a newfound resolve.

The brink of near-death experiences, unveiled in 2012, thrust me into an abyss of despair and resilience. Hospice papers, a stark reminder of mortality, intertwined with a resolve to defy prognosis. In the face of uncertainty, I sought solace, yearning for answers amidst the existential turbulence.

In the aftermath of that defining moment, I found myself ensnared in a complex web of existential questions. What lay beyond the threshold of life and death? Was there a realm beyond our mortal comprehension? These inquiries echoed within, urging me to seek solace amidst the overwhelming uncertainty.

Beyond the Veil:

A Journey Through Near Death Experiences

Each passing day became a testament to resilience, a silent vow to challenge the verdict of the hospice papers. Supported by an unwavering network of loved ones, their collective belief bolstered my determination to carve a path beyond despair.

The fragility of existence became a stark reality, overshadowed by a fervent desire to grasp onto hope. Moments of doubt collided with an unyielding resolve, a determination to rewrite the destiny charted by medical professionals.

Amidst the tumultuous journey, I was drawn to the enigmatic realm of near-death experiences, seeking solace and understanding amidst the turmoil. The brushes with mortality had woven a collage of emotions, unveiling the delicate balance between life's fragility and the resilience of the human spirit.

Echoes of those pivotal moments reverberated, intertwining with an insatiable quest for answers. The encounter with the threshold of mortality had ignited a yearning—a yearning to comprehend the inexplicable, to find meaning amidst the chaos, and to embrace the fragility of existence with a newfound reverence.

The relentless pursuit of understanding propelled me to delve deeper into the narratives of those who had traversed the precipice between life and death. Their accounts resonated, each story a mosaic of ethereal encounters, profound insights, and a transformative journey that defied conventional understanding.

In those narratives lay a common thread—a glimpse into a realm that transcended the constraints of our mortal comprehension. The luminous embrace of light, encounters with departed loved ones, and panoramic life reviews formed a kaleidoscope of experiences that resonated with an otherworldly significance.

Yet, amidst the celestial narratives, questions lingered—questions that eluded the grasp of rationale, questions that probed the very essence of existence. What lay beyond the veil of mortality? Was there a purpose woven into the fabric of these ethereal encounters?

The pursuit of understanding became a voyage of introspection, a journey that traversed the realms of spirituality, science, and the ineffable mysteries of life and death. It was a quest fueled by an insatiable thirst for knowledge, a yearning to unravel the enigma shrouding near-death experiences.

As I navigated this maze of inquiry, I discovered a profound truth—a truth that transcended the boundaries of empirical evidence and ventured into the realms of belief and

Beyond the Veil:
A Journey Through Near Death Experiences

personal revelation. It was the realization that the significance of near-death experiences lay not only in their ethereal encounters but in the transformative impact they bestowed upon those who traversed that sacred threshold.

These encounters, shrouded in mystique, served as catalysts for profound introspection, catalyzing a metamorphosis of perspectives, beliefs, and the very essence of being. They became mirrors reflecting the profundity of existence, inviting contemplation on the intricate web of life, mortality, and the elusive realms that lie beyond.

Through the prism of near-death experiences, I gleaned a deeper understanding—a realization that amidst the frailty of our mortal existence, there exists a realm of transcendence, a realm that beckons us to ponder the mysteries of our existence with reverence and awe.

In the echoes of those ethereal encounters, I found solace—a solace that transcended the confines of physicality and resonated with a deeper understanding of the interconnectedness of life, mortality, and the enigmatic journey that awaits us all.

The hospice papers, once a harbinger of finality, became a testament to the resilience of the human spirit—a reminder that within the darkest moments lie the seeds of unwavering determination and a fervent yearning for the mysteries that lie beyond the threshold of mortality.

As I traverse the vicissitudes of life, those defining moments continue to echo—a reminder of the fragile balance between mortality and the ethereal realms that beckon with their tantalizing mysteries. They stand as silent sentinels, inviting contemplation, and fostering a profound reverence for the inexplicable wonders that await us in the journey beyond.

The impact of morphine-induced stupors on consciousness:

In the realm of grappling with relentless pain, morphine emerged as a double-edged sword. It offered a fleeting escape from the unyielding agony, yet its embrace plunged me into a realm of altered consciousness—a space where the boundaries between reality and the ethereal blurred into an enigmatic dance.

These morphine-induced stupors became interludes in the theater of consciousness, moments when time bent and contorted. Linear progression became an elusive notion, slipping away like sand through fingers. In one such hazy interlude, I found myself in the luminous presence of my

Beyond the Veil:

A Journey Through Near Death Experiences

departed uncle, Jorge, a figure brimming with reassurance and love.

Morphine, with its tranquilizing effects, acted as a bridge, ferrying my consciousness into uncharted waters. It was within these states that I encountered Uncle Jorge, his message an anchor amidst the swirling currents—a conviction that whispered of unfinished chapters, a purpose yet unfulfilled on this earthly stage.

These encounters, born from the nebulous realms of morphine-induced consciousness, challenged the very fabric of my reality. They beckoned me into a quest, a quest to unravel the mysteries that shroud the threshold between life and the beyond. They became catalysts, propelling me into the exploration of near-death experiences and their profound impact on the human spirit.

The impact of these experiences, forged in the crucible of altered consciousness, reverberates far beyond mere hallucinations or fleeting delusions. While the medication veiled my perception, it also granted glimpses into an alternate reality, one that pulses parallel to our familiar existence. These encounters etched emotional imprints, bestowing solace, kindling hope, and reigniting the flame of resilience.

Amidst our pursuit of understanding near-death experiences, it's vital to approach these encounters with a mind unshackled from preconceptions. They offer gateways to realms beyond our grasp, prompting us to ponder the mysteries that swirl between life and death.

Yet, these experiences transcend the individual, often birthing profound personal growth and spiritual awakening. They challenge our perceptions, nudging us to reconsider the vast composition of consciousness that extends beyond the corporeal realm.

As we embark on this expedition into the recesses of near-death experiences, let us not merely approach it with intellectual curiosity. It is a journey that demands introspection, inviting us to confront mortality's delicate dance and contemplate the structure of our existence.

In the chapters that unfurl, we'll delve into the narratives and anecdotes of those who straddled the edge of life and returned. We'll dissect the common threads that weave through these experiences, seeking truths that may reshape our understanding of life's enigmatic essence.

But this isn't a mere exploration of esoteric tales. It's an invitation to a transformative odyssey—one that encourages us to reevaluate our convictions, embrace the inexplicable, and fathom the depths of our potential.

So, let's embark together on this expedition beyond the realm of the unknown. Let's unravel the enigma that veils near-death experiences and discover the profound verities that lay within. It's an opportunity to traverse the boundaries of existence and glean insights that illuminate the intricate corridors of consciousness itself.

Chapter 2: Encountering Uncle Jorge

I n the surreal embrace of my near-death experience (NDE), a realm where reality intertwined with the ineffable, I encountered a figure that transcended the confines of earthly existence—my beloved Uncle Jorge.

Uncle Jorge had been an anchor of wisdom and steadfast support throughout my life. His untimely departure had left a profound void, a yearning for his counsel in moments of distress. Yet, in the celestial network of the NDE, there he stood—a luminous presence emanating warmth and reassurance.

This encounter wasn't happenstance. It held a significance that transcended the ethereal landscape. It was a juncture where the boundaries between the corporeal and the metaphysical dissolved.

As our connection deepened, Uncle Jorge's message resonated within the very core of my being. *"It's not your time. You still have more to do."*

His words, infused with profound meaning, pierced through the fabric of my consciousness. In that fleeting moment, a revelation unfolded—an understanding that my illness wasn't a sentence of finality but a chapter in the book of life. It became a catalyst, urging me to tap into reservoirs of fortitude and resilience that lay dormant within.

Uncle Jorge's presence during my NDE became a catalyst for transformation. His message became an anthem of resilience, echoing through the corridors of my spirit. It ignited a flame within me—a determination to confront my illness with firm tenacity.

From that celestial encounter sprang a new perspective. I no longer viewed my illness as an insurmountable obstacle but as a crucible for personal growth. Uncle Jorge's words became a guiding beacon, illuminating a path strewn with challenges, yet brimming with the promise of victory.

The belief in his message became a cornerstone of my resolve. Armed with his wisdom, I approached my battle against illness with unwavering determination. It marked the genesis of a transformative journey where adversities weren't hurdles to lament but stepping stones toward resilience and empowerment.

His spectral visitations, whether a manifestation of my subconscious or a spiritual communion, served as a constant reminder that the bonds of love transcend the boundaries of mortality. His words became my armor—a source of strength that fortified me against the onslaught of despair.

As I emerged from the plane of the NDE, Uncle Jorge's message remained etched in the sanctum of my soul. It propelled a transformation—a metamorphosis that extended beyond the physical realm into the depths of my psyche.

This metamorphosis reverberated across all facets of my life. It ignited a fire within me, driving me to adopt a holistic approach to healing. I embraced rigorous medical treatments, engaged in alternative healing practices, and made profound lifestyle changes, steering my journey toward wellness.

However, Uncle Jorge's guidance transcended physical healing. It fostered a profound shift in my mental and emotional landscape. I cultivated a mindset rooted in gratitude and resilience, finding solace in the smallest moments and refusing to succumb to the shadows cast by adversity.

His spectral presence continued to grace my consciousness, guiding me through the peaks and valleys of my healing voyage. With each encounter, his message resonated, reinforcing my resilience and infusing me with unwavering strength.

Reflecting on the transformative encounter with Uncle Jorge during my NDE, gratitude swells within me. His presence didn't merely alter the trajectory of my battle against illness; it became the catalyst for a paradigm shift in my approach to life.

I learned that adversity, though daunting, harbors the seeds of growth. Uncle Jorge's message illuminated the path toward resilience, teaching me that the human spirit is capable of extraordinary feats.

As I traverse this labyrinthine journey of healing and self-discovery, Uncle Jorge's words echo as a perpetual anthem—a testament to the indomitable human spirit and the uncharted reservoirs of strength that reside within.

Chapter 3: The Unseen World Revealed

I n the immersive journey through the ethereal realm of my near-death experience, the hidden facets of existence unfurled before my eyes. Vivid colors danced with an unparalleled vibrancy, casting a gentle, luminous glow across this otherworldly domain. It transcended the bounds of the physical, merging time and space seamlessly into a symphony of harmony.

Amidst this mystical landscape, Uncle Jorge materialized, his presence exuding an ageless radiance. His countenance bore the etchings of wisdom surpassing mortal years, while his eyes shimmered with an understanding that transcended the mysteries of life's veil. His serene demeanor offered reassurance, as if he were a seasoned traveler in this ethereal plane.

Here, time seemed malleable, devoid of its earthly constraints. Uncle Jorge's form defied the rigidity of temporal bounds, a blend of youthful vitality and accrued wisdom. It felt as though his essence had distilled into a form embodying the eternal spirit.

In this realm, perception took on new dimensions. The limitations of physical senses dissolved, revealing an interconnectedness that pulsed with vibrant energy. It was as though a veil lifted, exposing a tapestry of energies intricately interwoven, resonating deeply within.

Further exploration revealed familiar yet unrecognized individuals, emanating an aura of affection and recognition, fostering a sense of kinship. They appeared familiar, akin to long-lost companions reunited in this realm beyond the physical.

Like Uncle Jorge, these enigmatic figures transcended the constraints of time and age. Their forms hinted at earthly existence, yet their essence bore knowledge surpassing mortal bounds. Their presence spoke of unity and interconnectedness, a reminder of our entwined existence in the fabric of the universe.

Their mysterious presence evoked curiosity—what roles had they played in my life, both in the physical and beyond? They hinted at a complex network of connections stretching far beyond conscious awareness.

In this realm where the unseen world unveiled its secrets, I began to comprehend the intricate web of existence. Here, age held no dominion, perception surpassed physical confines, and love's bonds traversed time and space.

As my journey in the NDE continued, I sensed glimpses of a reality beyond life's veil—hinting at infinite possibilities and eternal truths. Each moment deepened my understanding that this unseen world held the key to unraveling the mysteries of our existence and purpose within the cosmic tapestry.

Here, time flowed as a fluid continuum, merging past, present, and future into a cohesive whole. It felt as though the fabric of existence unfurled simultaneously, revealing the interplay of cause and effect across lifetimes. Time, as comprehended before, was but a fragment within a greater cosmic order.

Upon returning to my earthly self, I realized these unrecognized yet familiar souls were testament to the intricate weaving of our journeys through existence. Their presence, though unrecognized in their earthly forms, reminded me of soul connections transcending physical recognition.

This revelation enveloped me in profound tranquility. The unseen world, with its timeless interconnectedness, illuminated a deeper understanding of life's purpose—a realization that our earthly journey is a fragment within a grander cosmic odyssey, where lessons and connections resonate eternally.

The encounters with Uncle Jorge and these enigmatic beings reshaped my perception of life and death, stirring within

Beyond the Veil:

A Journey Through Near Death Experiences

me an awareness of interconnectedness and a yearning to delve into existence's depths. They highlighted that our journey extends beyond the physical realm and that the universe's mysteries await discovery.

With each step in this mystical realm, my connection to life's divine tapestry deepened. The unseen world unveiled itself as a realm of boundless potential where love, wisdom, and unity reign supreme. As I readied myself to return to the realm of the living, I carried with me the certainty that this unseen world would forever shape my perspective, infusing my journey with purpose and wonder.

Further exploration revealed that this unseen world wasn't solely a realm of beauty and interconnected souls. It was a realm rich with profound knowledge and spiritual growth. Encounters with Uncle Jorge and these beings became gateways to profound teachings and revelations.

I learned that the unseen world spanned multiple dimensions, encompassing diverse levels of consciousness and vibrational frequencies. Souls traversed these dimensions, driven by spiritual growth and the lessons they sought. It was a perpetual cycle of expansion and evolution, each soul's journey unique yet interwoven with the collective journey of all beings.

As my sojourn through the unseen world neared its close, a profound sense of gratitude and awe-filled me for the revelations and teachings bestowed. The encounters with Uncle Jorge and these beings expanded my consciousness and deepened my comprehension of existence.

Carrying the wisdom gained from this unseen world, I returned to the realm of the living, forever transformed.

Chapter 4: The Afterlife Journey

As I delved deeper into the phenomenon of near-death experiences (NDEs), I discovered a wealth of research and accounts from individuals who had encountered similar experiences in the realm beyond life. These stories provided remarkable insights into the nature of the afterlife and the purpose of NDEs.

I'm a doctor who studied 5K near-death experiences — there is life after death.

A radiation oncologist in Kentucky who has studied more than five thousand near-death experiences believes his research has proven the existence of life after death — "without a doubt."

Dr. Jeffrey Long founded the Near-Death Experience Research Foundation in 1998, having become fascinated with near-death experiences (NDE) while completing his medical residency.

Reflecting on these experiences in a recent essay for Insider, he defined NDEs as episodes where individuals, either comatose or clinically deceased, undergo a lucid state, engaging in sensory perceptions and interactions, despite the absence of vital signs. Gathering firsthand accounts and subjecting them to scientific analysis has been the cornerstone of my work.

While each NDE is a unique tapestry, Long discerned recurring motifs. Remarkably, around 45% of patients recount an out-of-body occurrence, where they describe their consciousness detaching from their physical form, often hovering above and observing their surroundings—a phenomenon corroborated by supporting witnesses.

One compelling incident involved a woman who lost consciousness while riding a horse. Her consciousness appeared to accompany her horse back to the barn. Remarkably, she later recounted the events at the barn, despite her physical absence.

Further accounts describe journeys into alternate realms, characterized by traversing tunnels, encountering radiant beings, reuniting with departed loved ones, and reliving life events—experiences that, though termed cliché, are echoed even by young children unfamiliar with these stories.

Despite exhaustive scrutiny, Long found no scientific explanation for these encounters, underscoring the depth and breadth of these reports.

Dr. Long's research aligns with the work of Dr. Bruce Greyson, a professor emeritus at the University of Virginia. His

Beyond the Veil:
A Journey Through Near Death Experiences

personal encounter with NDEs spurred a deep dive into their study. Despite extensive exploration of brain research and potential explanations, neither Greyson nor Long have found any plausible rationale for NDEs, pointing to something beyond the physical body. Yet, he has traced <u>a few similar traits</u> between some NDEs.

Consistent with his observations, NDEs, while not universal, are reasonably prevalent, reported by approximately 10-20% of those nearing death—approximately 5% of the general populace.

Moreover, many individuals he had encountered describe out-of-body experiences, encounters with radiant lights, and reunions with departed loved ones—a convergence of experiences that challenges conventional beliefs about the limitations of our physical existence.

"The evidence overwhelmingly points to the physical body not being all that we are," he shared with <u>The Post</u> in 2021. "There seems to be something that is able to continue after the body dies. I don't know what to make of it."

Despite these revelations, the profound mystery persists, leaving me grappling with the enigma of what lies beyond.

Stories of NDEs

True NDEs from individuals:

1. Upon awakening from my time on life support, I made the impulsive decision to remove the tube from my throat, unaware of my surroundings and mistakenly believing I was choking. To my surprise, I found myself engaged in conversations with unseen individuals surrounding my hospital bed. This peculiar phenomenon persisted even after my release, spanning approximately six months. During this period, my grip on reality seemed to waver intermittently. Although no words were exchanged, I somehow comprehended their inquiries on a telepathic level. Sometimes, I responded within my mind, while other times, my replies escaped audibly until I regained full awareness of my environment. As my healing progressed and my strength returned, these interactions gradually diminished and eventually ceased. Yet, during those bewildering times of uncertainty, unsure if I would survive, their presence provided a profound sense of solace. Although I never laid eyes on them, the tranquility they brought forth remains a cherished memory that I now yearn for.

Beyond the Veil:

A Journey Through Near Death Experiences

2. As I emerged from the depths of unconsciousness, my senses gradually returned, revealing a shocking revelation. In the confines of my hospital room, I found myself in the company of five ethereal beings. Their presence was palpable, as if a veil between realms had been momentarily lifted. Eager to share this extraordinary encounter, I beckoned a passing nurse named Nancy, who seemed perplexed by my conversation with invisible visitors.

Summoning my strength, I pointed toward the translucent figures and uttered the simple word, "Them." Nancy's bewildered gaze shifted from me to the wall, back and forth, unable to perceive what lay before me. With a mix of curiosity and doubt etched across her face, she mustered the courage to speak, "There's no one there."

Determined to provide undeniable proof, I turned my attention to the towering male presence among my spectral companions. Sensing his willingness to comply, I made a request, my voice filled with a combination of hope and desperation, "If it's within your power, please, make a sound against the window."

With a measured stride, the enigmatic figure moved toward the window, as anticipation filled the air. And then, with an otherworldly force, three resounding bangs echoed through the room, causing the entire glass panel to tremble as if on the verge of shattering. Startled, the nurse dropped her clipboard. Her eyes widened with disbelief. Overwhelmed by the intensity of the moment, she fled from the room, disappearing from my life entirely during the remainder of my hospital stay.

In the days that followed, I contemplated the significance of this inexplicable encounter. Were these unseen companions mere figments of my imagination, conjured by a mind on the threshold between life and death? Or were they emissaries from a realm beyond our mortal comprehension, sent to guide and comfort me during my most vulnerable hours?

Regardless of the answer, their presence instilled within me a profound sense of connection and reassurance. Their ethereal whispers echoed through my being, reminding me that even in the darkest of times, I was not alone. As I embarked on the arduous path of recovery, their benevolent influence remained etched in my memory, a beacon of light that would forever guide my way.

Beyond the Veil:
A Journey Through Near Death Experiences

3. In the depths of my memories, there exists a profound moment shrouded in uncertainty—a time when I traversed the realms that lie between life and death. The haze of drug-infused nights in the vibrant decade of the 80s clouds my recollection, blurring the line between reality and the realm of dreams. It was during one such episode that I believe I encountered an otherworldly experience, perhaps an NDE.

Whether it was a vivid hallucination or a genuine encounter with the unknown, I cannot be certain. In the depths of my slumber, I found myself astride a motorcycle—an unfamiliar vehicle in my waking life. The wind whipped through my hair as I accelerated, hurtling towards an ancient stone wall. The adrenaline coursing through my veins heightened my senses, and amidst the rush, a breathtaking sight caught my eye—a bed of radiant yellow flowers.

In an instant, the collision was upon me. The impact was tremendous, my body hurtling towards the wall at an unimaginable speed. It was then that an extraordinary phenomenon unfolded before my eyes. As if in the presence of an out-of-body observer, I witnessed myself and saw my very soul emerge from its earthly vessel—a phenomenon often referred to as the "third person" perspective. A resounding pop reverberated through the void, signifying the separation of my soul from my physical form.

Enveloped by a profound darkness, a sense of trepidation washed over me. In a matter of mere seconds, my soul recoiled in fear, snapping

45

back into its corporeal home. And then, as if emerging from a deep slumber, I awoke, drenched in perspiration, the remnants of an ethereal encounter lingering upon me. The memory etched itself into the recesses of my consciousness, an indelible mark upon my journey.

In the days that followed, I sought understanding, yearning to unravel the mysteries of that fateful night. It was revealed to me that the resounding pop I had heard was the very moment my soul liberated itself, severing ties with its mortal casing. In that fleeting instant, however, I inadvertently damaged the protective shield that guards the ethereal essence within us— the etheric shield.

Though the origin and nature of my experience remain uncertain, it served as a catalyst for profound introspection. It ignited within me a thirst for knowledge and a quest to heal the fragments of my being. The realization that my soul had ventured beyond the boundaries of my physical form left an indelible mark upon my perception of existence.

In the tapestry of my life, this enigmatic encounter continues to whisper its secrets, urging me towards a deeper understanding of the interconnectedness of our spiritual and physical realms. It serves as a reminder of the delicate balance between the palpable and the unseen, and the eternal quest to mend the fragments of our souls as we navigate this extraordinary journey called life.

Beyond the Veil:

A Journey Through Near Death Experiences

4. Good day beautiful souls ❤. *My name is... In December of 1997 I had a near death experience. I was in a horrific car accident with my son and 2 nephews.*

The man that struck my vehicle sadly ran a stop sign. We were on our way to a holiday dinner celebration and my husband was in his truck right behind us who saw everything. When we were struck I started beeping the horn aggressively and when my husband approached the vehicle he saw that our son was bleeding and attended to him, rightfully so. My nephews were fine thankfully.

When I was hit I was in excruciating pain as my side of the vehicle crushed me and my left leg was stuck under the dashboard. I immediately realized that I couldn't expand my lugs/chest and couldn't breathe anymore. I then realized I couldn't feel any pain, and my entire life flashed before me, and every possible worry (like how my son would be taken care of without me).

Next thing I know I am in a very unfamiliar place, followed by seeing my body dead, eyes closed and not breathing. I had a strong sense of a request to look at my body where my head was to the left and my feet to the right and I am outside of my body looking at it, saying goodbye to the physical body I was in. I looked around and I literally saw infinity with no end at sight. I immediately upon entering felt the absolute most pure peacefulness which there is nothing on earth to even begin to express or experience. I immediately started looking all around and was graciously shown so much and given a wealth of information and knowledge.

After receiving all this information, I started to turn to the left about 35-40 percent as if I was continuing on to somewhere else. Next thing I know I am in an ambulance and telling the paramedics that I can not breathe, they kept reassuring me that I was because I actually spoke to them and to keep breathing.

Next I was in the trauma unit with so many doctors and nurses all over me. My husband informed me that they kept telling him that they are trying to stabilize me and not sure if they can. My husband was running back and forth between me in the trauma unit and my son in the emergency room. My son was later discharged and recovered fully.

While it took them 6 hours or so to stabilize me and gratefully they did, I did have to stay in the hospital for a bit. I ended up having to go through at least 10 years of rehabilitation, aquatic therapy ect. and suffered going through, roughly 50 surgeries due to all the damage and internal bleeding in my physical body.

The aftermath of dying and coming back took a very long time to process especially coming back with gifts I, at the time, couldn't understand. As I could see things that others weren't aware of, I could feel things that others couldn't. I then realized that I received incredible gifts. I could precisely connect to souls that have passed, my hands are able to heal, and through my hands I could preform medical intuition to the exact problem.

Beyond the Veil:

A Journey Through Near Death Experiences

Although I had to go through a lot to recover, I was blessed to be able to do mediumship work, perform medical intuition and help people that went to 10-20 doctors and still weren't doing well.

The fact that I can and have been able to give so many answers from their loved ones, give people their quality of life back (depending on the circumstances, within 3 months) no matter what trauma they are going through and answering on the medical intuition side is such a bigger blessing.

5. Hey so I have a few experiences that have really caused a lot of sadness and judgement in my life. They are out of the norm and not typical of OBE's and NDE's.

I went to hell a few times and Jesus got me out. Everytime I asked Him to get me out and I came back in my body. I told Him I would tell people what I experienced. I heard from other NDE'ers that we go to hell because we think we deserve it somehow and that it isn't a real plain. It felt like a dream that felt very real that I couldn't wake up from. I couldn't wake up no matter how hard I tried and the only way out was to talk to God. I am not sure if I died or not In these experiences. I woke up from them in pain and gasping for air.

So yeah idk, I usually go places in my sleep as well. I have some good experiences too. I had an OBE where I fell asleep listening to the song El Shaddai and I came out of my body and there was a bright white cross shining throughout me, it was all love and all joy. I can't describe the love and joy I felt. It was powerful and electric. It looked like lightening or stars.

Years before all these experiences when I was a kid, I went swimming in the ocean and there was a red flag on the beach telling us not to go into the water, I followed my dad and his friend out there. I got stuck in the rip tide and couldn't get out. I was calling for help but no one could hear me because the wind was so strong that day. I got taken under and every time I would try to come up for air another wave would take me under

Beyond the Veil:
A Journey Through Near Death Experiences

until I was just spinning under the waves. I came out of my body and felt a lot of peace and thought wow dying isn't that bad.

Then I remembered the story about the 2 mice that fell into a vat of milk one gave up and drowned and the other kept swimming until it churned butter and crawled out. Then it was this thought that was like which mouse are you going to be. I went back into my body and started swimming parallel to the shore toward the sound of a small child playing on the shore. And I lived.

What are you alls thoughts on these experiences? I won't go into detail about the hell experiences they are really traumatizing and there are probably a lot of triggers in them. I wonder if I went to hell because I thought I deserved it or if it was Bc God wanted to show it to me, or if I actually deserved it. What do you guys think? People have been very rude to me about my experiences because it's not what they want to hear.

6. I was having surgery to correct some issues I was having with scar tissue from previous surgeries. My body tended to over process and cause the scar tissue to grow and wrap or attach to my internal organs.

Due to my beliefs and previous history, I signed a DNR order before all my surgeries as I figure if I'm meant to return to the spirit world, I didn't want anyone wasting time trying to bring me back, if it's my time it's my time. But I was pretty sure that wouldn't be the case since I've known since I was Eleven yrs. old my assigned death date. But since I have had quite a few conversations with 'I Am' and have offered to trade in some of my time here in exchange for others to have a little more time here, in order to make arrangements to take care of things. But again, that's another story for another time.

So, I was having surgery, when suddenly I flat lined, and the machines hooked up to me were making a loud sound. The nurse brought the defibrillator to the side of the operating table and the doctor told her there was no need, that I had signed a DNR, to which she said I was way too young and didn't have any medical reason to not try to save me. (I was 41 at that time)

Before my surgery I had a meeting with psychiatrist to make sure I was of sound mind, as he said I didn't have a serious illness so why my request for a DNR form. Anyway, to cut a long story short I satisfied him that I was of sound mind and body and didn't have depression or anything else to cause him to deny my request. In layman's terms I don't have a death wish, but I don't have a strong desire to remain in this world

Beyond the Veil:
A Journey Through Near Death Experiences

longer than is absolutely necessary, as I said been dead before, so don't have a fear of it, because life in the spirit is by far more than most understand it to be.

So, at the time the machines were sounding off my lack of heartbeat and blood pressure, I was watching the scene from a place up above the room. I again felt the great spirit's presence and then saw it, we were as before in the spirit and conversing without need for voices. I had a few more questions and was told as before that often the questions asked by those freshly out of the body were not relevant to the spirit world. (Needless to say, I didn't get those questions answered) The spirit world doesn't have anything similar to that of earth, what bothered people here on the planet didn't relate in anyway to those in the spirit. I did ask what I could see as spirit that I couldn't see from earth. 'I Am' laughed and took me to see different realms, nine in all, star patterns, planets unlike any I'd seen here. Beautiful colours and amazing sights, there is life on many other planets, waterfalls, oceans some a very different colour from our own. Planets with skies that look like a rainbow, one had what looked like a live moving sky that reminded me of the seas movement.

At the same time as seeing those realms, I also was watching what was happening in the operating theater, I heard the discussion between the doctor and nurse. He was quite sharp with her as she tried several times to talk him into using the paddles. At the position I was in I could see the back of her neck; I saw she had a strawberry birthmark just at her hairline and only noticeable because she had a cap on for the surgery. If I had been laying awake on the table I wouldn't have been able to see it, but because of where I was in the spirit it was clearly visible to me.

'I Am' and I spoke for what seemed like hours to my recollection of our conversation but was only approx. twelve minutes in earth time. Like I said before to many there is a huge difference in how time is in the spirit and how it is on the planet. It's kind of like having a dream were it seems like hours and is maybe only a few minutes to thirty minutes in real dream time.

I again asked 'I Am' if it was possible for me to stay in the spirit, that I felt so happy, and so much love there, I also felt my spirit felt able to stretch and wasn't cramped like in the body. But was again told it wasn't my time, that I wasn't done with why I was placed here. I asked again how come I had to be in this body, it was too small for my spirit, 'I Am' laughed and said "by the time you leave it, you will have just gotten used to it, keep banking love and share when your spirit leads you to share what you know, what you see, and hear from the spirit world, things they can't see but you can."

At that moment I felt that sudden rush taking me back to the body lying on the table and I heard the doctor's voice. "We have her back, she said if she wasn't meant to die, she would either get through this surgery fine or the spirit would send her back, guess it threw her back. (I heard him chuckle and the nurse make a sound like she didn't get it at all.)

Beyond the Veil:

A Journey Through Near Death Experiences

Let's finish up here and get her into recovery, we need to bring her temperature back up, have the blankets ready."

I went under again and heard nothing else until I was waking up freezing cold and shivering like crazy as another heated blanket was piled on top of me. They felt like a heavy weight on me, eight blankets in all at that time. I believe I had a total of twelve blankets on me by the time all was said and done.

In the doctor's office a week later I spoke with him about what I saw and heard while I was clinically dead, his nurse was like. "You were dreaming maybe, you couldn't possibly have seen anything, your mind was probably just sparking thoughts." The doctor didn't agree with her, especially when I said about her birthmark. He said he had heard several patients tell of things they shouldn't have known but did know because they had a view of what was going on when they were supposed to be dead, or at very least totally under anesthetic.

While in the spirit as before I felt a freedom, a loving all around me, an ability to multitask if you will, talking, listening, seeing, knowing in every direction. To be in multiple places all at the same time, there was never any fear or apprehension, there was always that feeling of being home and totally happy.

7. I never thought that a simple trip to the grocery store could change my life so drastically. It was just an ordinary day, and I was going about my usual routine as a middle-aged, heavyset single man. Little did I know that this would be the day I would come face to face with my mortality.

I remember stepping into the store, feeling a strange tightness in my chest. At first, I brushed it off as stress or indigestion. But as I made my way through the aisles, the discomfort intensified, spreading to my arms and jaw. Panic set in as I realized something was terribly wrong.

Before I knew it, darkness consumed me. I had collapsed in the middle of the store, my body succumbing to a sudden cardiac arrest. Time became a blur as I drifted in and out of consciousness.

During those moments of unconsciousness, a peculiar sensation washed over me. It was as if I was floating, weightless and detached from my physical body. I could see a bright light in the distance, beckoning me forward. Curiosity mingled with fear as I moved closer to the ethereal glow.

As I approached the light, a profound sense of peace enveloped me. I felt an overwhelming presence, a loving energy that embraced me without words. It was as if I was being held in the gentlest of hands, cradled and comforted. The worries and pain of my earthly existence melted away, replaced by a profound serenity.

In that timeless realm, I found myself reliving moments from my past, both joyful and painful. I saw the impact I had on others, the relationships

Beyond the Veil:
A Journey Through Near Death Experiences

I had nurtured, and the moments of kindness I had shared. It was a bittersweet reflection, reminding me of the beauty and fragility of life.

But just as I began to settle into this surreal state, a voice echoed through the void, pulling me back. It was distant at first, barely audible, but soon it grew louder and more urgent. The voice called out to me, urging me to return, to fight against the darkness.

I resisted. The allure of that serene realm was almost too tempting to resist. But the voice persisted, becoming more insistent. It was as if a lifeline had been thrown to me, and I had a choice to make.

With a surge of determination, I willed myself to return. I felt a sudden jolt, a rush of energy surging through me. I gasped for breath, my body convulsing as life returned to my veins. The darkness receded, replaced by the blinding fluorescent lights of the grocery store.

I was surrounded by a group of concerned faces, strangers who had come to my aid. They told me that they had performed CPR on me, their actions giving me a second chance at life. Tears welled up in my eyes as gratitude flooded my heart. I was overwhelmed by the realization of how close I had come to losing everything.

Since that near-death experience, my perspective on life has changed in profound ways. I no longer take anything for granted. Every day is a gift, an opportunity to cherish the beauty and wonder that surrounds me.

I've learned to appreciate the small joys, the laughter of loved ones, the warmth of the sun on my face, and the taste of a delicious meal. I've become more present, more connected to the people and world around me.

I often find myself wondering about that ethereal realm I glimpsed during my near-death experience. It remains etched in my memory, a reminder of the profound love and peace that awaits us beyond this earthly existence. It has given me a newfound sense of purpose, a deeper understanding of the interconnectedness of all things.

In the months that followed my cardiac arrest, I embarked on a journey of self-discovery and renewal. I sought out ways to improve my health and well-being, embracing a healthier lifestyle with regular exercise and a balanced diet. I became more attuned to my body's signals, prioritizing self-care and stress management.

But beyond my physical well-being, I also nurtured my spiritual side. I delved into books on meditation and mindfulness, seeking solace and guidance in the practice of quieting my mind. I found a sense of peace in those moments of stillness, a connection to something greater than myself.

My near-death experience had a profound impact on my relationships as well. I reached out to old friends, mended broken bonds, and fostered new connections. I realized the importance of human connection, the power of love and support in navigating the ups and downs of life.

I also became more attuned to the needs of others. Knowing firsthand the fragility of life, I sought opportunities to lend a helping hand, to be a

Beyond the Veil:
A Journey Through Near Death Experiences

source of comfort and compassion for those in need. Whether it was volunteering at a local shelter or simply offering a listening ear to a friend, I found solace in acts of kindness.

Life, once mundane and routine, now felt vibrant and full of possibilities. Each day held the potential for growth, for learning, and for making a positive impact on the world around me. I embraced new experiences with an open heart, stepping out of my comfort zone and embracing the unknown.

Today, as I reflect on my near-death experience, I am filled with gratitude for the second chance I have been given. It serves as a constant reminder to live each day to the fullest, to appreciate the beauty and wonder that exists in every moment. I no longer fear death, for I have caught a glimpse of the love and peace that lie beyond.

My journey is far from over, and I know there will be challenges along the way. But armed with the lessons I learned during my near-death experience, I face the future with courage and resilience. And as I continue to navigate the twists and turns of life's path, I hold onto the belief that every experience, both joyous and painful, is an opportunity for growth and transformation.

I am forever changed by that fateful day at the grocery store, by the darkness and the light that I encountered. And with each passing day, I strive to honor the gift of life I have been given, embracing it fully and embracing the possibility of a brighter future.

Beyond the Veil:

A Journey Through Near Death Experiences

8. I woke up to blinding lights and the faint sound of beeping machines. Disoriented and groggy, I tried to move, but my body felt heavy and unresponsive. Panic washed over me as I realized something was terribly wrong. I strained my eyes, struggling to make sense of my surroundings. That's when I saw them—the doctors and nurses, their faces etched with worry, huddled around a tiny bundle.

Suddenly, memories flooded back, and I remembered the excruciating pain, the desperate struggle to bring my child into this world. But then, everything went dark. It was as if time had stopped, and I was hovering above my own lifeless body, witnessing the scene unfold before me.

The medical team worked tirelessly, their hands moving swiftly and deliberately. Their faces were a mix of determination and concern. I watched as they fought to revive me, their efforts fueled by a sense of urgency. But it wasn't just me they were fighting for. My heart ached as I saw them tending to my newborn baby girl, her tiny body so fragile and vulnerable.

Through the haze, I could hear their voices, a symphony of urgency and hope. They shouted orders, their words blending together, but their meaning was clear—they were fighting for both of us. The realization hit me like a ton of bricks. I couldn't leave my child, not now, not when she needed me the most.

I pleaded silently, willing my lifeless body to respond. I wanted to hold my daughter, to comfort her, to be the mother she deserved. The seconds stretched on, each one feeling like an eternity. And then, a flicker of movement—a twitch of my finger. Hope surged through me as I willed every ounce of strength into that tiny motion.

The medical team noticed the sign of life, and their efforts were redoubled. They fought with renewed determination, refusing to give up on me. As their efforts intensified, I felt a surge of energy coursing through my veins. The darkness that had enveloped me began to recede, replaced by a warm, glowing light.

I watched as the doctors and nurses exchanged looks of relief, their faces brightening with joy. They had done it. They had brought me back from the brink of death. Tears streamed down my face as I realized the gift that had been given to me—a second chance at life, a chance to be the mother my daughter needed.

Time blurred as I returned to my body, my senses awakening once again. The room swam into focus, and I saw the medical team standing around me, their faces a mix of exhaustion and triumph. And then, the sweetest sound reached my ears—the cry of my baby girl. I turned my head, and there she was, nestled in the arms of a nurse, her tiny face scrunched up in protest.

I would forever carry the memory of that near-death experience, a reminder of the fragility and preciousness of life. But I would also carry the strength and resilience that had brought me back, a testament to the love and dedication of those who fought for our lives. The days that followed

Beyond the Veil:
A Journey Through Near Death Experiences

were a whirlwind of emotions, as I recovered from the trauma of childbirth and marveled at the miracle of my daughter. The medical team continued to monitor us closely, ensuring that we both received the care we needed.

As I regained my strength, I couldn't help but feel a profound gratitude towards the doctors and nurses who had fought so hard to bring me back. I wanted to express my heartfelt appreciation to each and every one of them, to let them know the impact they had made on our lives. So, once I was well enough, I sought them out.

I began to express my gratitude, my voice filled with emotion. I thanked them for their skill, for their unwavering dedication, and for their belief in the power of life. Tears welled up in their eyes as they listened, their own emotions palpable. It was a bittersweet moment as we reflected on the fragility of life and the resilience of the human spirit.

As my daughter grew, I often found myself reflecting on the near-death experience I had gone through. It served as a constant reminder of the preciousness of life and the strength that lies within us, waiting to be awakened in the face of adversity. I vowed to live each day with gratitude, cherishing the moments and embracing the love that surrounded me.

My daughter, now a vibrant and curious toddler, would never fully understand the incredible journey we had been through together. But she would always know the strength of a mother's love, the unwavering devotion that had brought us back from the edge. And I, too, would never *forget the medical team who had fought for us, who had given us a second chance at life.*

Beyond the Veil:

A Journey Through Near Death Experiences

9. I lay still on the cold, sterile hospital bed, my heart pounding in my chest. At thirty-five years old, I never imagined I would be there, preparing for bypass surgery. The doctors had assured me that it was necessary, that it would give me a chance at a longer and healthier life. But as I looked up at the bright lights above me, doubts and fears crept into my mind.

The doctors and nurses moved around me, their faces masked by concentration. I closed my eyes, trying to find solace amidst the chaos. That's when it happened.

Suddenly, a profound sense of peace washed over me, enveloping me in its warm embrace. I felt weightless as if my body had become disconnected from the physical world. And then, I saw it — a blinding light, more radiant than anything I had ever witnessed before. It beckoned me, drawing me closer with its ethereal glow.

As I ventured toward the light, the hospital room faded away, replaced by breathtaking landscapes. I found myself surrounded by vibrant colors, lush greenery, and flowers in shades that seemed impossible. It was a scene of unparalleled beauty, like stepping into a dream.

But what truly took my breath away were the angelic beings that materialized before me. They emanated an otherworldly aura, their presence calming and comforting. Their eyes sparkled with wisdom and love as they gently guided me through the events of my past life. I saw the joys and sorrows I had experienced, the moments that shaped me into the person I am today.

Time seemed to lose all meaning in this realm. I felt a profound connection to everything around me, a unity with the universe itself. It was a place beyond pain, beyond worry, and beyond fear. I yearned to stay, to bask in the serenity that enveloped me.

But just as I started to settle into this newfound paradise, one of the angelic beings turned to me with a tender smile. Their voice was like a gentle breeze, murmuring in my ear, "It is not your time, dear one. You have more to do in the world below."

Reluctantly, I understood. I had unfinished business, a purpose yet to be fulfilled. With a heavy heart, I reluctantly began my journey back, feeling the warmth and light slowly fade away. The landscapes and angelic beings became distant memories, slipping away as if they were mere fragments of a dream.

When I opened my eyes, I was back in the sterile hospital room, the beeping of machines filling my ears once again. It took a moment for my mind to register the transition, to comprehend that I had been given a glimpse of something extraordinary.

As the days turned into weeks, and my body healed from the surgery, I carried the memory of that experience deep within me. It was a reminder of the beauty that lay beyond this physical existence, a reminder that life is a precious gift, meant to be cherished and lived to the fullest.

Beyond the Veil:
A Journey Through Near Death Experiences

I still long for that world I glimpsed, the world of radiant lights and peaceful beings. But for now, I know I have a purpose, a reason to be here. And as I embark on this new chapter of my life, I carry with me the profound knowledge that there is more to our existence than what meets the eye.

But as time passed, the memory of my encounter began to fade. Life's demands pulled me back into its relentless grip, and the extraordinary soon became a distant echo. Yet, a flame had been ignited within me, a yearning for a deeper understanding of the mysteries of life.

I became more attuned to the beauty that surrounded me in the everyday moments. The laughter of children in the park, the gentle touch of a loved one's hand, the vibrant hues of a sunset — these simple joys seemed to carry a newfound significance. I started to recognize the interconnectedness of all beings, sensing a divine presence in every breath I took.

But there were moments when the weight of the physical world bore down on me, and I longed for the serenity I had tasted. In those moments, I would close my eyes, allowing my mind to drift back to that realm of light and beauty. I would remember the angelic beings who had guided me, their wisdom and love transcending all barriers.

And so, I lived my life as a bridge between these two worlds, carrying the memory of that near-death experience within me like a guiding light. I knew that one day, when my time came to depart this world, I would be reunited with the angelic beings and the radiant landscapes that had captivated my soul.

But until then, I would continue to honor the beauty and wonder of life, savoring each moment as a precious gift.

Beyond the Veil:
A Journey Through Near Death Experiences

10. I woke up disoriented and drenched in sweat. My heart pounded against my chest, its rhythm erratic and wild. Slowly, my surroundings came into focus, revealing the bright nightlights of the street. The paramedics hovered over me and my mother, crying. It was at this moment that I realized I had survived something unimaginable—a terrifying near-death experience.

As the fog in my mind cleared, memories flooded back, piercing my consciousness with a jolt of regret and fear. My name is Alex, and I was once an innocent adolescent who had fallen into the clutches of a dangerous addiction. Drugs had entangled me in their deceptive grip, promising me an escape from my problems while gradually consuming my very soul.

The night it all happened was a blur—a hazy blend of euphoria and despair. My desperation to escape the reality of my life had led me to that fateful moment when I crossed the line, carelessly consuming a deadly cocktail of substances. It was a gamble I had no idea I was taking, and it nearly cost me everything.

As my body succumbed to the toxic concoction, a darkness enveloped me. I was no longer in the sidewalk of my parents home but transported to a realm that seemed to exist between life and death. The air was heavy with an otherworldly silence, and an ominous chill crept down my spine.

Attempting to gather my bearings, I looked around and found myself standing on a desolate path. The scenery was a twisted reflection of reality—bare trees reached out with gnarled branches, their skeletal forms casting eerie shadows upon the ground. A gray mist shrouded everything, obscuring any sense of direction.

Fear tightened its grip on me as I stumbled forward, each step feeling like a struggle against an invisible force. Whispers echoed in the air, unintelligible voices that seemed to come from all directions. Panic swelled within me like a storm, threatening to consume me completely.

Suddenly, a figure emerged from the mist. Its appearance was a translucent silhouette that seemed to radiate both warmth and power. As it drew closer, I recognized the figure as a person, yet something ineffable set it apart from any ordinary individual.

Their voice resonated through my very being, gentle yet commanding. "Alex, you stand at the precipice of your choices. This path you have chosen leads to destruction. But it is not too late. You have the power to change."

Tears welled up in my eyes as a profound sense of regret washed over me. At that moment, I saw the devastation I had inflicted upon myself and those who cared for me. The pain etched upon their faces, the shattered pieces of trust that I had left in my wake—it all became a painful reality that I could no longer ignore.

With a trembling voice, I pleaded, "Please... help me. I want to change. I want to live."

Beyond the Veil:

A Journey Through Near Death Experiences

The figure's presence radiated compassion, wrapping me in a warmth that defied the icy grip of the mist. "The journey will not be easy, but it is possible. Seek out those who can guide you, who can help you rebuild what has been broken. You are stronger than you realize, Alex. Embrace your second chance."

As their words echoed in my soul, I felt a surge of hope rising within me. I knew that the path to recovery would be arduous, paved with challenges and temptations. But I also understood that I had been given a rare opportunity—a chance to reclaim my life and rewrite my story.

Gradually, the mist began to dissipate, revealing glimpses of light and color. The figure faded away, leaving me standing alone on the path, but I was no longer afraid. Determination coursed through my veins, replacing the numbness that had consumed me for far too long.

Back in my own body, I opened my eyes with newfound clarity. I was filled with gratitude for the medical professionals who had fought to save me, for my family who had never given up on me.

Recovery would not be a solitary journey. I knew I needed support, guidance, and unwavering love. I reached out to my loved ones, laying bare my struggles and committing to a path of healing. Their response was overwhelming—teary embraces, words of encouragement, and a shared determination to walk alongside me every step of the way.

In the weeks and months that followed, I immersed myself in rehabilitation programs, therapy sessions, and support groups. I surrounded myself with individuals who understood my struggles and offered unwavering support. Together, we shared stories of hope, resilience, and strength that emerged from the darkest corners of our lives.

Every day was a battle, but each small victory fueled my determination. I rebuilt broken relationships, mended trust, and rediscovered my own worth. I learned to forgive myself for the mistakes of the past and to focus on the present moment, knowing that my future was being shaped by each choice I made.

Years have passed, and my life has been transformed in ways I could never have imagined. I pursued my passions, found purpose in helping others, and live each day with gratitude. The memory of that terrifying near-death experience never faded completely; it remained a constant reminder of the fragile balance between life and the choices we make.

I had journeyed from the depths of despair to a place of healing and hope. My scars served as a testament to my resilience, a reminder of the battles I had fought and the strength I had discovered within myself.

And as I stood on the solid ground of my newfound life, I pledged never to forget the lessons learned in that otherworldly realm. I would carry the weight of my past, not as a burden, but as a reminder of the person I had been and the person I have become.

Beyond the Veil:

A Journey Through Near Death Experiences

RECURRING THEMES

In my exploration of these accounts, certain themes continually emerged, revealing glimpses into the profound nature of near-death experiences (NDEs). Among these recurring motifs, one prevalent theme was the overwhelming sense of peace and serenity that enveloped individuals during their NDEs. Many vividly described a feeling of weightlessness, a detachment from their physical body, as they journeyed into the unknown. The transition from life to the afterlife often unfolded in the presence of a radiant light, emanating warmth and love, drawing them toward an unknown reality.

Equally common were encounters with deceased loved ones or spiritual entities. These experiences were often vivid and lifelike, fostering a profound sense of connection and understanding. Greeted by departed relatives or spiritual guides, individuals found comfort and guidance during their journey. These encounters often left an indelible mark, fundamentally altering their perspectives on life and death.

Furthermore, numerous accounts detailed traversing through a tunnel or gateway, emerging into an otherworldly realm beyond earthly comprehension. This vibrant landscape, rich with unimaginable colors and profound harmony, transcended the bounds of time and space. It seemed a place where conventional constraints dissolved into an expansive realm of knowledge and understanding.

As I delved deeper into the nature of the afterlife, questions about the purpose of these experiences surfaced. What significance did they hold? Why were individuals granted a glimpse into the realm beyond life, only to be returned to their earthly existence?

Various perspectives emerged regarding the purpose of NDEs. Some proposed that these experiences acted as a bridge between the physical and spiritual realms, offering profound opportunities for growth and learning. They suggested these encounters expanded our comprehension of interconnectedness and reminded us of the boundless potential within the human spirit.

Others hypothesized that NDEs offered reassurance and solace to those approaching the end of their earthly journey. By glimpsing the afterlife, individuals shed their fear of death, embracing a deeper understanding of the eternal nature of the soul.

However, contrasting views suggested NDEs might be a manifestation of the brain's response to trauma or oxygen

Beyond the Veil:

A Journey Through Near Death Experiences

deprivation. While acknowledging the profound impact on individuals' lives, this perspective attributed these experiences solely to physiological processes.

Amidst these diverse viewpoints, I realized the purpose of NDEs might be as varied as the individuals who experienced them. Perhaps there was no singular answer to this profound mystery, and only those who had undergone such experiences could truly comprehend their significance.

In subsequent chapters, I sought to delve deeper into these multifaceted perspectives, exploring the scientific, spiritual, and philosophical dimensions of NDEs. Through examination of evidence and personal accounts, I aimed to illuminate the nature of the afterlife and the purpose behind these profound encounters, inching closer to understanding the ultimate journey awaiting us all.

As my research progressed, I discovered that the exploration of the afterlife and the purpose of NDEs extended far beyond individual experiences. Scientists, philosophers, and theologians dedicated their lives to unraveling the mysteries surrounding these profound phenomena.

Scientific studies aimed to provide rational explanations, focusing on physiological and neurological processes during near-death situations. Theories suggesting hallucinations or the brain's attempt to comfort in the face of death gained traction, yet failed to explain the consistent patterns present in countless NDE accounts.

In contrast, spiritual and religious perspectives offered alternative lenses. Many religious traditions held beliefs in an afterlife or realms beyond earthly existence, aligning with NDEs and providing glimpses into described realms in sacred texts.

Life reviews emerged as an intriguing aspect of NDEs. Individuals reported panoramic replays of their lives, witnessing significant events and feeling the emotions of those impacted by their actions. This phenomenon prompted reflections on life's purpose, love, compassion, and forgiveness.

Some suggested life reviews served as spiritual purification and growth, facilitating introspection and the cultivation of wisdom, preparing souls for continued spiritual evolution.

Encounters with a higher power or divine presence were equally intriguing. Individuals described profound love and connection, often perceiving a reunion with a supreme being or universal consciousness. These encounters instilled a deep

Beyond the Veil:

A Journey Through Near Death Experiences

understanding of interconnectedness and imbued life with purpose and meaning.

The purpose of NDEs might transcend scientific inquiry and religious belief. These experiences could catalyze personal transformation and remind us of the eternal nature of the soul. They offer glimpses into a reality beyond our physical existence, inviting exploration of life's profound questions.

As I concluded my exploration of the afterlife journey and the purpose of NDEs, I realized that while definitive answers might elude us, these experiences hold immense value in expanding our understanding of the human experience. They challenge us to contemplate existence and interconnectedness, offering hope and reassurance in something greater beyond the material world.

Chapter 5: Life's Purpose and Second Chances

F ollowing the haunting echoes of my own brush with mortality and the profound implications revealed through extensive research, a panorama of transformation unfolded within me. The encounter with the precipice of life and the mysterious dimensions beyond had etched an indelible tattoo upon my soul, infusing it with resilience, tenacity, and a persistent sense of purpose. It was as though the universe had granted me a reprieve, an opportunity to craft a profound legacy from the shards of my own existence.

In the fabric of time, 2017 arrived like a clarion call to awaken. A singular morning unveiled itself with startling clarity, as though a shroud had been lifted, revealing the roadmap of my raison d'être with steadfast certitude. Inspired by the celestial concordance of love and empathy I had encountered in the ether, I embarked upon a pilgrimage to leave an indelible mark upon the world.

"Angeles Para Honduras" blossomed forth from the depths of this transformative odyssey—an endeavor born not just from the echoes of my near-death encounter but from a recognition of unfinished endeavors. As I treaded the ethereal

Beyond the Veil:
A Journey Through Near Death Experiences

corridors between life and the beyond, a solemn realization dawned upon me: life was not solely about individual pursuits but an unspoken covenant to illuminate the lives of the less fortunate.

The tempestuous temerity of NDEs paints a composition that surpasses conventional understanding. They unfold vistas that shatter the shackles of perception, presenting us with a riddle that defies the confines of the tangible world. It is not merely the visual tableau that captivates, but the very essence— the symphony of sensations that paint the canvases of these extraordinary experiences.

Akin to an artist transcending the mundane with surreal brushstrokes, these moments envelop one in a celestial embrace. The radiant luminescence that eclipses earthly radiance bathes the spectral landscape with an ethereal warmth—an embrace exuding an ineffable love that defies quantification.

Yet, the narrative unfurls beyond mere ethereal vistas. Departed souls, etched in memory, stride through the veils of existence, bridging the chasm between worlds. A montage of life is unveiled—an introspective reel where every heartbeat, every choice, every emotion reverberates with profound resonance, transcending the confines of the ordinary.

The echoes of these encounters sculpt souls in ways that the limitations of language falter to encapsulate. Priorities metamorphose, beliefs reshape, and vistas shift in seismic tremors that redefine the fabric of our existence. It's this transformation, this chrysalis of the spirit, that etches the profound significance of near-death encounters. They beckon us to ruminate upon the ineffable nature of being, the enigma of life's ephemerality, and the tantalizing prospect of realms beyond perception.

June 8th, 2012, marked the genesis of an unforeseen expedition, steering my life's trajectory into uncharted waters. A routine surgical endeavor at the University of Vermont Medical Center morphed into a chaotic tangle of unforeseen tribulations, an unanticipated saga of despair and resilience.

In the hallowed corridors of the operating room, an unseen storm brewed amidst my unconscious repose. Oblivious to the imminent tumult, the ensemble of beeping monitors and the sterile ambiance cocooned me in a surreal sanctuary.

Days bled into an eternity, each passing moment a precarious tightrope walk between existence and oblivion. The medical entourage waged a valiant battle to anchor me to life, each heartbeat a silent testimony to the relentless skirmish.

Beyond the Veil:
A Journey Through Near Death Experiences

Then arrived the cataclysmic moment, its resonance etched in the contours of despair. Dr. Neil Hyman, his somber countenance a harbinger of bleak tidings, painted a dire panorama. My fortress, the liver, had turned traitor, unleashing chaos within—a whirlwind of sepsis ensnaring my fragile vessel.

Weeks slithered by in a harrowing blur, a cacophony of pain and relentless procedures. Tubes snaked within, draining the venomous bile that sought to consume my essence. It was a duet of agony, a relentless duel against time and the unrelenting tide of illness.

Each moment etched upon my form a narrative of anguish, a testament to the crucible my body had endured. Returning home, the familiar embrace concealed the unseen battle scars, a testament to the silent turmoil that had ravaged my being. Gaunt and fragile, the reflection in the mirror bore witness to a saga etched in the flesh.

Chapter 6: Integration and Healing

As the odyssey from the precipice of existence draws to a close, a new narrative unfurls—an epoch of assimilation and restoration. Near-death encounters (NDEs) stand as pivotal junctures, sculpting an indelible imprint upon one's soul, urging a profound fusion of newfound wisdom with the rhythms of ordinary existence. Let's have an expedition through the aftermath of an NDE, navigating the terrain of readjustment post such a transcendental rendezvous, and embracing the wisdom gleaned to nurture restoration across the realms of physical, emotional, and spiritual well-being.

Coping with the Aftermath

Upon reentry from an NDE, individuals often find themselves entangled in a whirlwind of emotions and musings that overwhelm the senses. Confronting the brink of mortality and the enigma of what lies beyond leaves an enduring imprint upon the fabric of the mind. It's paramount to recognize that navigating the aftermath is an intimate journey, unique to each soul, given the deeply personal nature of the experience. Nonetheless, amidst this puzzle, there exist shared strategies to traverse this intricate phase.

Beyond the Veil:

A Journey Through Near Death Experiences

1. **Embracing Support:** Forging connections with kindred spirits who've traversed similar ethereal realms can offer solace beyond measure. Support groups, virtual communities, and tailored counseling services catering to NDEs can provide sanctuaries for mutual understanding, empathy, and solidarity.

2. **Delving into Reflection:** Crafting a chronicle through journaling, capturing the intricacies of the NDE and the spectrum of emotions post-experience, serves as a compass for navigating and assimilating this journey. Contemplating the wisdom gained and reliving those poignant moments becomes an act of both healing and enlightenment.

3. **Nurturing the Self and Practicing Patience:** Nurturing the self through rituals of care—be it meditation, physical activity, communing with nature, or embracing creative expressions—becomes a conduit for healing and self-revelation. Equally vital is the virtue of patience, allowing the integration of such a profound encounter to unfold in its own time within the backdrop of one's life.

Adjusting to Life After an NDE

The reintegration into quotidian existence following an NDE stands as a formidable endeavor. The encounter invariably reshapes one's outlook, recalibrating perspectives, recalculating priorities, and altering the very fabric of understanding. Navigating this metamorphosed reality mandates a delicate equilibrium—a fusion of imbibed teachings with the pursuit of normalcy.

1. **Reassessing Priorities:** The revelations unearthed amid an NDE often prompt a profound reassessment of life's hierarchies. Relationships, career trajectories, and personal aspirations undergo scrutiny, transformed by this catalytic moment of growth and renewal.

2. **Cultivating Present Awareness:** Embracing the current moment and nurturing mindfulness serve as a bridge linking the extraordinary echoes of the NDE with the mundane rhythms of daily existence. Practices such as meditation, conscious breathing, and deliberate immersion in daily rituals anchor individuals in the immediacy of the now.

3. **Disseminating Enlightenment:** Many NDE survivors feel an impassioned yearning to disseminate the newfound wisdom garnered from their ethereal sojourn. This impulse drives them to write, speak, or engage in communal endeavors, sharing their insights to illuminate others. In this act of sharing, not only do they aid fellow voyagers but also deepen their own assimilation and comprehension of the NDE's essence.

Healing Physical, Emotional, and Spiritual Aspects

NDEs imprint a profound resonance upon the physical, emotional, and spiritual facets of one's essence. Rejuvenation in these realms necessitates a comprehensive approach, recognizing the intricate interplay among these dimensions.

1. **Physical Restoration:** Post-NDE physical healing entails addressing any corporeal ailments or injuries incurred during the ethereal encounter. Seeking medical guidance, adhering to treatment regimens, and embracing a wholesome lifestyle bolster the body's recuperative journey. Practices like yoga, tai chi, and energy-based healing modalities aid in reinstating equilibrium and vitality to the physical form.

2. **Embracing Emotional Wholeness:** The emotional ripples post-NDE carry immense weight. It's common to traverse a spectrum of emotions—awe, gratitude, confusion, and even apprehension. Engaging in therapy or counseling provides a sanctuary for navigating and processing these emotional landscapes. Healing emotionally also encompasses the realms of forgiveness—both of oneself and others—alongside nurturing self-compassion and acceptance.

3. **Integration of Spirituality:** NDEs often ignite profound spiritual awakenings, fostering a deep connection beyond the self. Infusing these spiritual facets into daily existence involves exploring diverse spiritual practices like meditation, prayer, or contemplative rituals. Meaningful dialogues and seeking guidance from spiritual mentors enrich the assimilation of these experiences into life's tapestry.

4. **Unveiling Meaning and Purpose:** The aftermath of near-death encounters often unveils a heightened sense of purpose, a fervent desire to impact the world positively. Unearthing and aligning with one's life purpose becomes a transformative odyssey, entailing exploration of personal values, engagement in meaningful endeavors, and nurturing relationships fostering personal growth and fulfillment.

5. **Sustained Evolution and Learning:** Post-NDE healing transcends into an ongoing evolution—a perpetual voyage of growth and learning. Embracing an open-minded approach and a willingness to delve into new realms of comprehension and self-exploration is pivotal. Participation in personal development endeavors, attending workshops, and seeking novel experiences further underpin this journey of continual growth and amalgamation.

Post-NDE, the voyage of integration and healing unfolds as an intimate and metamorphic odyssey. Through the application of coping mechanisms, acclimatization to a life enriched by newfound wisdom, and the nurturing of physical, emotional, and spiritual domains, individuals traverse the aftermath of an NDE with grace and fortitude. The fusion of these extraordinary encounters into the substance of daily existence holds the promise of profound restoration, burgeoning personal evolution, and a rekindled beacon of purpose.

Chapter 7: The Ripple Effect

The profundity of near-death experiences (NDEs) outstrips the solitary facets of the experiencer. As these narratives are disseminated, they possess the potency to initiate ripples, extending their reach to touch the souls of others, eliciting profound shifts in their perceptions. Let's explore the expansive influence of sharing NDE anecdotes—a catalyst for instilling hope, fostering resilience, and igniting profound dialogues concerning the essence of life, mortality, and the elusive pursuit of purposeful existence.

Delving into the Impact of Shared NDE Stories

1. **The Power of Storytelling:** Revealing one's NDE story requires bravery and openness. Through these personal accounts, individuals glimpse dimensions that transcend our conventional comprehension of existence. These narratives possess an innate ability to captivate, resonating deeply with others, sparking a quest to delve into the enigmatic realms of life and mortality.

2. **Validation and Connection:** Shared NDE stories offer validation to those who've undergone similar experiences, dispelling isolation and fostering understanding. These shared chronicles forge connections, affirming a

collective journey beyond the ordinary, bestowing solace and empowerment upon both storytellers and listeners.

3. **Expanding Perspectives:** NDE narratives challenge established norms, pushing the boundaries of human cognition. By sharing these experiences, individuals prompt others to reconsider assumptions about life, death, consciousness, and reality itself. This sharing fosters a culture of inquisitiveness, broadening horizons and inviting exploration into the mysteries of existence.

Fostering Hope and Fortitude

1. **Transcending Fear of the Unknown:** Near-death experiences often uncover a profound sense of tranquility, love, and interconnectedness. Through the dissemination of these encounters, individuals sow seeds of hope, assuaging the pervasive dread of death in societies. NDE narratives prompt a paradigm shift, beckoning individuals to embrace mortality as an inherent facet of human existence, fostering a richer, more present-oriented life.

2. **Nurturing Resilience:** Within NDE anecdotes, resilience and inner fortitude often gleam amidst transformative narratives. Sharing these stories becomes a beacon, kindling the flame within others to draw upon their

inner reservoirs, navigating life's tribulations with valor and poise. These tales serve as beacons, reminding us that resilience is not just attainable but an intrinsic facet of our being.

3. **Cultivating Personal Evolution:** NDE narratives spotlight the significance of self-growth, introspection, and the pursuit of a purposeful existence. By sharing these encounters, individuals ignite a spark within others, urging them to embark on their paths of self-discovery and metamorphosis. These stories act as catalysts, igniting a fervor to explore one's essence, values, and latent capabilities.

Discussions on Life, Death, and the Meaning of Existence

1. **Initiating Dialogue:** NDE narratives reveal avenues for profound conversations delving into life's existential inquiries. Through shared experiences and insights, individuals delve into discussions encompassing consciousness's enigma, life's purpose, and the existential meaning. These dialogues cultivate a deeper comprehension and reverence for the myriad human experiences and beliefs.

2. **Voyage through Spiritual and Philosophical Realms:** Within NDE anecdotes reside glimpses of spiritual and philosophical scopes, nudging individuals to traverse diverse ideologies and belief structures. By fostering open-

minded exchanges, individuals delve into multifaceted spiritual doctrines, philosophical ideologies, and interpretations surrounding life and mortality. These discussions nurture a collective treasury of wisdom, fostering mutual respect and tolerance.

3. **Unveiling Significance and Direction:** NDE narratives beckon individuals to scrutinize their own narratives, pondering the deeper significance and direction underlying their existence. By engaging in conversations encompassing life, death, and the essence of existence, individuals unearth clarity, inspiration, and a revitalized sense of direction. These dialogues propel individuals toward intentional living, harmonizing actions with values, and fostering positive global impact.

4. **Fostering Emotional and Spiritual Well-being:** Meaningful exchanges concerning life, death, and the afterlife offer solace, comfort, and hope to those grappling with grief, loss, or existential quandaries. These conversations foster supportive environments, allowing individuals to articulate their thoughts, fears, and aspirations, nurturing emotional and spiritual harmony.

The reverberations emanating from the sharing of NDE stories surpass individual experiences. Through the narration of these extraordinary encounters, individuals become beacons, kindling hope and fortitude in others, initiating dialogues about life, mortality, and existential profundity, and igniting an impetus for personal evolution and exploration. Harnessing the potency of storytelling and candid exchanges, NDE narratives possess the potential to catalyze profound transformations in perspectives, cultivating connectivity and comprehension, and instilling a fervor within individuals to embrace life's abundance with purpose and depth.

Chapter 8: Beyond Death's Door

As we stand on the threshold of mortality, our thoughts inevitably turn to what lies beyond. Throughout history, humanity has grappled with the mysteries of the afterlife, seeking answers to questions that defy our understanding. Near-death experiences (NDEs) offer a unique glimpse into the dimension beyond death's door, providing compelling insights into what might await us on the other side.

Exploring the Possibilities of the Afterlife

Near-death experiences, frequently recounted by individuals who've teetered on the brink of death yet returned, have enraptured the intrigue of scientists, philosophers, and spiritual seekers alike. These narratives commonly share recurring themes, such as sensations of departing the body, traversing through a tunnel, encountering departed loved ones, and basking in an overwhelming sense of serenity and affection.

While skeptics argue that NDEs stem from physiological and psychological processes, others perceive them as compelling evidence pointing towards an afterlife. These encounters often propel individuals to ponder the essence of reality and the potential existence of a higher field. Could it be that NDEs expose glimpses into the framework of existence, extending far beyond our earthly bounds?

Cultural and Religious Perspectives on Near-Death Experiences

Near-death experiences are not confined to cultural and religious boundaries, permeating diverse societies across history. Yet, the interpretations and depictions of these transcendent encounters often diverge, shaped by cultural and religious convictions.

In certain Western cultures, NDEs are often recounted as journeys through a tunnel toward an illuminating radiance, mingling with departed kin or revered religious entities. Conversely, specific Eastern traditions accentuate the concept of reincarnation, portraying the soul's passage through myriad realms before embarking on a new life.

Religious perspectives on near-death experiences exhibit variance as well. Some religious doctrines, like Christianity, construe NDEs as glimpses into heavenly or hellish domains, fortifying beliefs in an afterlife and divine judgment. Conversely, in traditions like Buddhism, NDEs are perceived as products of the mind, elucidating that ultimate reality surpasses the realms traversed in these encounters.

Contemplating the Nature of Consciousness and the Soul

Near-death experiences prompt profound inquiries into the essence of consciousness and the existence of the soul. If consciousness can exist independently from the corporeal form, does it imply that consciousness stands as an intrinsic facet of the universe? Furthermore, if the soul indeed exists, what defines its core essence and how does it intertwine with our individual identity?

Scientists and philosophers persist in grappling with these inquiries, endeavoring to forge connections between empirical observations and metaphysical spheres. Some postulate that consciousness emerges from intricate neural networks, while others contend that consciousness constitutes an innate element interwoven within the tapestry of reality itself.

Equally mysterious is the concept of the soul. Various suppositions suggest the soul as an eternal, immutable essence transcending physical demise, while alternate theories propose the soul as a dynamic, evolving entity undergoing metamorphosis and evolution across successive lifetimes.

The Intersection of Science, Spirituality, and Philosophy

As humanity delves deeper into the enigmas of consciousness and the afterlife, the convergence of science, spirituality, and philosophy emerges prominently. The study of near-death experiences serves as a bridge, providing glimpses into a reality that transcends the confines of scientific exploration alone.

Scientists have begun probing the physiological and neurological mechanisms underpinning NDEs, endeavoring to unravel the profundities nestled within these encounters. Breakthroughs in neuroimaging and consciousness studies offer valuable insights into brain function during near-death states, shedding light on potential operative mechanisms.

Simultaneously, spiritual and philosophical insights contribute to a broader comprehension of NDEs. They furnish interpretations surpassing the physical realm, delving into metaphysics, spirituality, and the essence of existence itself. These perspectives remind us of the multifaceted human experience extending beyond the confines of laboratory measurements and observations.

The intersection of science, spirituality, and philosophy facilitates a holistic exploration of the afterlife's mysteries.

Beyond the Veil:

A Journey Through Near Death Experiences

Rather than perceiving these disciplines as discrete and contradictory, an embrace of their complementary nature arises, each presenting distinct perspectives and insights.

In this integrated approach, openness surpasses rigid boundaries in the quest to explore the afterlife. It advocates for interdisciplinary collaboration, urging scientists, theologians, philosophers, and individuals with firsthand experiences to share their knowledge, beliefs, and conjectures.

Though definitive answers to the afterlife's queries may remain elusive, the exploration proves invaluable and enriching. It challenges our presumptions, enriches comprehension, and beckons us to contemplate the profound enigmas beyond the threshold of death.

Near-death experiences furnish a riveting aperture into the potentialities of the afterlife, offering fleeting glimpses of a reality transcending our corporeal existence. These encounters ignite contemplations surrounding consciousness's nature and the enigmatic essence of the soul. By examining these encounters through diverse cultural, religious, scientific, and philosophical lenses, we deepen our comprehension of the mysteries awaiting us beyond death's threshold.

John Dewane

The convergence of science, spirituality, and philosophy empowers us to approach these inquiries with open-heartedness and open-mindedness, embracing the splendor and marvel of the unexplored. As we persist in exploration, let us nurture receptivity to the possibilities that lie beyond, for it is within the pursuit of understanding that the bounds of human knowledge and perception expand.

Chapter 9: Embracing Life's Journey

C ontemplating the enigmas surrounding the afterlife and the profound narratives emerging from near-death experiences, it remains imperative to retain a keen awareness of the inherent value of the present life we lead. Amidst our explorations into the afterlife's mysteries, the living present unfolds as a realm where the pursuit of purpose, fulfillment, and a profound gratitude for the essence of existence can be authentically realized. While the afterlife provides a lens for introspection and reflection, it is within the vibrancy of current existence that the true potential for meaningful experiences beckons, encouraging us to delve into the richness of the living harbor that surrounds us.

Embracing Life's Marvels and Confronting its Trials

The distinctive viewpoint offered by near-death experiences serves as a poignant reminder of life's delicate nature and fleeting character. These encounters often act as catalysts, urging individuals to reassess their priorities, shedding light on the insignificance of trivial concerns, and embracing the profound aspects that hold genuine significance.

Rather than assuming the permanence of life, we are prompted to greet each day with appreciation and a sense of awe. Acknowledging the ephemerality of our existence, we can treasure our connections, pursue our passions, and uncover significance in the uncomplicated joys that envelop us.

Furthermore, integrating life's challenges into our journey becomes an indispensable component. Narratives of near-death experiences frequently recount the transformative influence of adversity and the wisdom acquired through confronting and triumphing over obstacles. Through the acceptance of challenges, we foster resilience, fortitude, and a more profound comprehension of our inner selves.

Implementing Insights Drawn from Near-Death Experiences

The profound lessons derived from near-death experiences have the potential to significantly shape the way we navigate our existence. Narratives of NDEs frequently underscore the significance of love, compassion, forgiveness, and the interconnectedness shared by all living beings.

By seamlessly incorporating these insights into our daily routines, we can nurture more meaningful connections, extend kindness to others, and foster a sense of harmony with the world that surrounds us. Actively prioritizing acts of service allows us to contribute to the well-being of others and aspire to leave a positive imprint on the lives we encounter.

Moreover, near-death experiences serve as poignant reminders of the importance of living authentically. They advocate for attentive listening to our inner voice, honoring our genuine desires and passions. Through aligning our actions with our true selves, we open ourselves to experiencing a profound sense of fulfillment and purpose.

Embracing Gratitude and Reverence for Every Instant

The practice of gratitude holds transformative potential in shaping our outlook on life. Near-death experiences frequently instill a profound sense of gratitude in those who undergo these extraordinary encounters, kindling an awareness and appreciation for the often overlooked blessings in our lives.

Nurturing gratitude enables us to attune ourselves to the inherent beauty of each passing moment. Through this practice, we learn to relish the modest joys, extract meaning from the commonplace, and acknowledge the interconnectedness weaving through all our experiences. Gratitude serves as a catalyst, redirecting our attention from what may be lacking to the abundance that is already present, fostering a deep-seated contentment and fulfillment.

Furthermore, living with an appreciation for every moment prompts us to be fully immersed in the present. It extends an invitation to practice mindfulness, encouraging us to engage wholeheartedly in the richness of our experiences. By savoring the current instant, we not only deepen our connection to life but also unearth profound joy in the simplest and most ordinary of moments.

Embracing Life's Odyssey

As we wholeheartedly embrace life's unfolding odyssey, we pay homage to the myriad experiences—both mundane and extraordinary—that intricately weave the fabric of our existence. The contemplation of the afterlife serves as a poignant reminder that, within the vast cosmic chronicle, our time on Earth is a limited and profoundly precious gift.

Through the acts of cherishing life, navigating its challenges, assimilating the wisdom from near-death experiences, and living with gratitude and appreciation, we embark on a transformative journey of self-discovery and continual growth. Life, rather than a fixed destination, reveals itself as an ongoing narrative of lessons, experiences, and opportunities for personal evolution.

Beyond the Veil:

A Journey Through Near Death Experiences

This odyssey compels us to release attachments to outcomes, embracing the undulating rhythms of existence. Challenges and setbacks are not hindrances but invitations for introspection and growth. Every encounter, whether joyous or painful, contributes to the intricate mosaic of our lives, unraveling insights into our essence and the boundless potential for transformation.

Cultivating self-compassion and self-care becomes imperative on this journey. Acknowledging our imperfections, vulnerabilities, and struggles, we learn, heal, and find resilience. Self-compassion entails extending the same kindness and understanding to ourselves that we would offer to a cherished friend navigating adversity.

Connections with others emerge as significant milestones, recognizing the profound influence of human relationships. Empathy, compassion, and attentive listening foster genuine connections, enabling mutual support through the challenges and triumphs of individual journeys.

Embracing life's journey transcends the quest for a final destination or definitive answers to life's mysteries. It invites us to relish the present, uncover joy and meaning in the immediate, and honor the interconnectedness shared by all living beings.

In the face of uncertainty, we approach life with curiosity, wonder, and an open heart. Acceptance prevails for aspects of existence that may elude comprehension, finding solace in the allure of mystery. The paradoxes and intricacies of life become avenues for profound wisdom and growth.

As we culminate this expedition, traversing the realms of near-death experiences and contemplating life's purpose, let us carry forward the lessons learned and insights gained. Each day is a gift—an ephemeral opportunity to explore, learn, love, and evolve. In traversing this extraordinary journey, may we uphold an appreciation for the beauty of existence, honor the interconnectedness binding all beings, and embrace the profound depths of our own souls.

Chapter 10: The Everlasting Connection

L ying in my hospital bed, my mind veiled by the effects of morphine, I found myself transported to a dimension beyond the physical realm. In this hazy state, my beloved Uncle Jorge, who had departed just months prior, appeared before me. His presence brought comfort and familiarity, and I sensed a profound purpose behind our meeting.

Uncle Jorge stood radiantly, exuding strength and vitality. Despite departing at 71, he appeared as a vibrant 40-year-old in this ethereal encounter. Dressed in a crisp white guayabera, black dress pants, and shiny black Florsheim shoes, he embodied the youthful energy that defined him.

More striking was the gathering of souls standing behind him. Unfamiliar faces, yet a strange warmth enveloped me— an inexplicable sense of long-lost companionship. They seemed like old friends, distant memories, yet their identities eluded me.

With a gentle smile, Uncle Jorge reached out, but before I could embrace him, he halted me. "It's not your time yet," he said, his voice a blend of love and urgency. "You still have much to do in this world."

His words echoed through me, resonating in my soul. This encounter wasn't a product of imagination or drug-induced visions—it was a profound spiritual connection, a message urging me to find strength and continue fighting my illness.

As consciousness returned, and my body healed, Uncle Jorge's words became my guiding light. The memory fortified me to face challenges, a reminder that my earthly purpose was yet unfulfilled.

In the following days, I sought solace in exploring the enduring bond with departed loved ones. Immersing myself in spirituality, I uncovered that the connection transcends death, transforming into something everlasting.

Through meditation, prayer, and introspection, I recognized signs and synchronicities—a delicate butterfly, a familiar song, a whisper in the wind—gentle reminders of their presence, watching from the spiritual realm.

Trusting intuition, I listened to subtle whispers for guidance. In moments of doubt, I'd close my eyes, seeking Uncle Jorge's wisdom and the collective wisdom of those behind him. Their presence comforted me, guiding me on the path ahead.

Time strengthened the bond between the physical and spiritual realms. Departed loved ones continued to exist in a dimension beyond comprehension, offering guidance, protection, and unconditional love.

My connection with Uncle Jorge and the souls behind him became a wellspring of inspiration and strength. Delving into spirituality, I recognized subtle energies, interpreting signs as messages from the other side.

Sharing experiences with those seeking solace, I discovered a universal network of connections between the physical and spiritual. Together, we explored the mysteries of life and death, realizing departed souls communicate through dreams, intuition, signs, and whispers.

Uncle Jorge's purpose, as alluded to in our encounter, extended beyond worldly obligations. It urged me to embrace my essence, live authentically, and positively impact others. The connection underscored the interconnectedness of souls and the importance of compassion, love, and kindness.

Guided by Uncle Jorge and spiritual support, I embarked on a journey of self-discovery and service. Their presence inspired me to overcome obstacles, embracing life's fullness.

The everlasting connection with Uncle Jorge and the departed souls shaped my existence. It served as a reminder that life, intricately woven with threads of love and connection, transcends time and space.

Reflecting on this remarkable journey, gratitude fills me for the enduring bond with departed loved ones. Their love and guidance inspire me, affirming that we're never alone, and connections extend beyond the physical realm.

In the depths of my soul, I carry the eternal flame of love and connection nurtured by Uncle Jorge and the gathering of souls behind him. As I navigate life's twists, I do so with the unwavering knowledge that love transcends barriers and our departed loved ones forever intertwine with our journey.

In the years following our ethereal encounter, I discovered the power of honoring departed memories. Rituals, reflections, and keeping spirits alive through photographs and stories provided solace, ensuring legacies endure.

Seeking a deeper understanding of the spiritual realm, I delved into ancient wisdom, connecting with like-minded individuals and communities fostering spiritual growth.

Recognizing the interconnectedness of existence, I understood that we're part of a greater whole, united by a shared purpose and interconnected by transcendent love.

Beyond the Veil:

A Journey Through Near Death Experiences

Through this realization, I found courage and strength to fulfill Uncle Jorge's spoken purpose. Embracing unique gifts and passions, I dedicated myself to making a positive impact, advocating for those grieving.

The connection with Uncle Jorge and the gathering of souls remained, manifesting in signs and synchronicities, affirming their presence and guidance. Their everlasting bond fueled resilience, wisdom, and hope.

As I look back, Uncle Jorge and the gathering of souls profoundly impacted my life. Their presence inspires intentional living, cherishing relationships, and embracing life's beauty and fragility.

In the loom of existence, the connection with departed loved ones is a thread weaving through every moment. It's a reminder that love is eternal, and even in physical separation, the bonds of the heart remain unbroken.

I walk forward, guided by the everlasting connection with Uncle Jorge and the gathering of souls. With gratitude and renewed purpose, I embrace life's beauty, knowing love transcends boundaries, forever entwined in the continuum of eternity.

Conclusion: Embracing the Unseen

In the depths of our human experience lies a realm of the unseen — an ethereal tapestry that intertwines the physical and the spiritual, the known and the unknown. It is within this realm that we discover the transformative power of near-death experiences (NDEs) and the profound connection we share with departed loved ones.

Through the stories of those who have journeyed to the other side and returned, we catch a glimpse of the mysteries that lie beyond the veil of our earthly existence. We are reminded that life is a sacred gift, meant to be cherished and embraced with open hearts and open minds.

The encounters with departed loved ones, like my own with Uncle Jorge, reveal a truth that extends far beyond the boundaries of our mortal understanding. They remind us that death is not an end but a transition — a doorway that leads to a realm where love and connection transcend time and space.

These experiences offer us solace and guidance, igniting a flame of hope and resilience within us. They teach us to listen to our intuition's whispers, recognize the signs and synchronicities that guide us and trust in the unseen forces that shape our lives.

Beyond the Veil:
A Journey Through Near Death Experiences

Embracing the mysteries of life and death requires courage—the courage to delve into our souls' depths, question our beliefs, and expand our consciousness. It is a journey that invites us to explore our existence's vastness and embrace the beauty of the human experience.

In this grand tapestry of life, we are offered limitless potential for growth and self-discovery. We are invited to recognize the interconnectedness of all souls, to cultivate compassion and empathy, and to live with intention and purpose.

As we navigate the ebb and flow of our earthly existence, let us remember the profound connections we forge with those who have passed away. Let us honor their memory, cherish their love, and carry their wisdom in our hearts.

May we find peace in the unseen, embracing the mysteries that lie beyond our comprehension. May we recognize the transformative power of NDEs and the everlasting bond that unites us with departed loved ones.

And may we, in our own unique ways, contribute to the tapestry of existence, weaving threads of love, compassion, and growth. In embracing the unseen, we discover the true essence of our humanity — the boundless capacity for connection, growth, and the eternal flame of love that forever burns within us.

Appendix: Additional Resources and Further Reading

This appendix provides a list of recommended books, memoirs, research papers, websites, support groups, and organizations dedicated to Near-Death Experiences (NDEs). These resources can offer further insights, personal accounts, scientific research, and support for those interested in exploring the topic in more depth.

Books and Memoirs on NDEs:

1. "Life After Life" by Raymond Moody

2. "Dying to be Me" by Anita Moorjani

3. "Proof of Heaven: A Neurosurgeon's Journey into the Afterlife" by Eben Alexander

4. "Embraced by the Light" by Betty J. Eadie

5. "Consciousness Beyond Life: The Science of the Near-Death Experience" by Pim van Lommel

6. "The Afterlife Experiments: Breakthrough Scientific Evidence of Life After Death" by Gary E. Schwartz

Research Papers on NDEs:

1. "AWARE—AWAreness during REsuscitation—A prospective study" by Sam Parnia et al. (2014)

2. "Near-Death Experience in Survivors of Cardiac Arrest: A Prospective Study in the Netherlands" by Pim van Lommel et al. (2001)

3. "Terminal Lucidity in Patients with Chronic Schizophrenia and Dementia: A Survey of the Literature" by Michael Nahm et al. (2011)

4. "Near-death experiences, consciousness, and the brain: A new concept about the continuity of our conscious minds" by Mario Beauregard and Denyse O'Leary (2012)

5. "Near-death experiences and the temporal lobe" by Kevin Nelson (2013)

Websites, Support Groups, and Organizations:

1. International Association for Near-Death Studies (IANDS) - www.iands.org

2. Near-Death Experience Research Foundation (NDERF) - www.nderf.org

3. The Near-Death Experience: Problems, Prospects, Perspectives (NDE-PPP) - www.near-death.com

4. The Forever Family Foundation - www.foreverfamilyfoundation.org

5. Near-Death Experience Support - www.near-death.com/support.html

6. Near-Death Experience Research Foundation Forum - www.nderf.me

Please note that while these resources provide valuable information and support, it is essential to approach the topic of NDEs with an open and critical mind. The field of NDE research is still evolving, and the interpretation of these experiences remains a subject of debate among scientists, philosophers, and religious scholars.

It is also recommended to consult peer-reviewed scientific journals, attend conferences, and engage in discussions with experts in the field to stay updated on the latest advancements in NDE research.

Remember that personal experiences and individual interpretations of NDEs can vary significantly, and it is important to respect and consider diverse perspectives when exploring this subject matter.